When buying canvas, you may find that some canvas is firm and rigid while other canvas is softer and more pliable. To decide which type of canvas is right for your project, think of how the project will be used. If you are making a box or container, you will want to use firmer canvas so that the box will be sturdy and not buckle after handling. If you are making a tissue box cover, you will not need the firmer canvas because the tissue box will support the canvas and prevent warping. Softer canvas is better for projects that require a piece of canvas to be bent before it is joined to another piece.

AMOUNT OF CANVAS
The project supply list usually tells you how much canvas you will need to complete the project.

When buying your canvas, remember that several different manufacturers produce plastic canvas. Therefore, there are often _____ in canvas, such as differe_____ _____ a small difference _____ ariations, try to buy e_____ _____ oject at the same ti_____ _____ it is always bette_____ _____ ve leftovers tha_____ _____ re you finish your project. _____ _____ _____ extra canvas, you not only allow for _____stakes, but have extra canvas for practicing your stitches. Scraps of canvas are also excellent for making magnets and other small projects.

LESSON #2
SELECTING YARN

You're probably thinking, "How do I select my yarn from the thousands of choices available?" Well, we have a few hints to help you choose the perfect yarns for your project and your budget.

TYPES OF YARN
The first question to ask when choosing yarn is, "How will my project be used?" If your finished project will be handled or used a lot, such as a coaster or magnet, you will want to use a durable, washable yarn. We highly recommend acrylic or nylon yarn for plastic canvas. It can be washed repeatedly and holds up well to frequent usage and handling. If your finished project won't be handled or used frequently, such as a framed picture or a bookend, you are not limited to washable yarns.

Cost may also be a factor in your yarn selection. There again, acrylic yarn is a favorite because it is reasonably priced and comes in a wide variety of colors. However, if your project is something extra special, you may want to spend a little more on wool yarn to get certain shades of a color.

The types of yarns available are endless and each grouping of yarn has its own characteristics and uses. The following is a brief description of some common yarns used for plastic canvas.

WORSTED WEIGHT YARN - This yarn may be found in acrylic, wool, wool blends, and a variety of other fiber contents. Worsted weight yarn is the most popular yarn used for 7 mesh plastic canvas because one strand covers the canvas very well. This yarn is inexpensive and comes in a wide range of colors. Worsted weight yarn has four plies which are twisted together to form one strand. When the instructions call for "2-ply" or "1-ply" yarn, you will need to separate a strand of yarn into its four plies and use only the number of plies indicated in the instructions.

SPORT WEIGHT YARN - This yarn has three thin plies which are twisted together to form one strand. Like worsted weight yarn, sport weight yarn comes in a variety of fiber contents. The color selection in sport weight yarn is more limited than in other types of yarns. You may want to use a double strand of sport weight yarn for better coverage of your 7 mesh canvas. When you plan on doubling your yarn, remember to double the yardage called for in the instructions too. Since sport weight yarn must be doubled to completely cover 7 mesh canvas, you may prefer to use other types of yarns.

TAPESTRY YARN - This is a thin wool yarn. Because tapestry yarn is available in a wider variety of colors than other yarns, it may be used when several shades of the same color are desired. For example, if you need five shades of pink to stitch a flower, you may choose tapestry yarn for a better blending of colors. Tapestry yarn is ideal for working on 10 mesh canvas. However, it is a more expensive yarn and requires two strands to cover 7 mesh canvas. Projects made with tapestry yarn cannot be washed.

PERSIAN WOOL - This is a wool yarn which is made up of three loosely twisted plies. The plies should be separated and realigned before you thread your needle. Like tapestry yarn, Persian yarn has more shades of each color from which to choose. It also has a nap similar to the nap of velvet. To determine the direction of the nap, run the yarn through your fingers. When you rub "with the nap," the yarn is smooth; but when you rub "against the nap," the yarn is rough. For smoother and prettier stitches on your project, stitching should be done "with the nap" *(Fig. 5)*. The yarn fibers will stand out when stitching is done "against the nap" as shown in **Fig. 6**. Because of the wool content, you cannot wash projects made with Persian yarn.

Fig. 5

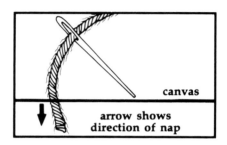

canvas

↓ arrow shows direction of nap

Fig. 6

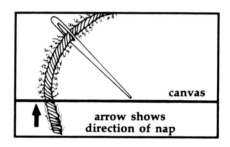

canvas

↑ arrow shows direction of nap

PEARL COTTON - Sometimes #3 pearl cotton is used on plastic canvas to give it a dressy, lacy look. It is not meant to cover 7 mesh canvas completely but to enhance it. Pearl cotton works well on 10 mesh canvas when you want your needlework to have a satiny sheen. If you cannot locate #3 pearl cotton in your area, you can substitute twelve strands of embroidery floss.

EMBROIDERY FLOSS - Occasionally embroidery floss is used to add small details such as eyes or mouths on 7 mesh canvas. Twelve strands of embroidery floss are recommended for covering 10 mesh canvas. Use six strands to cover 14 mesh canvas.

NUMBER OF STRANDS

The chart below gives the number of strands recommended to cover 7 mesh, 10 mesh, and 14 mesh canvas. Yarn is not recommended to cover 5 mesh canvas.

Type Of Yarn	7 mesh	10 mesh	14 mesh
Worsted Weight	1 or 2	1	nr*
Sport Weight	2 or 3	1	nr*
Tapestry Yarn	2 or 3	1	nr*
Persian Yarn	3 or 6	3	2
#3 Pearl Cotton	1 or 2	1	nr*
Embroidery Floss	nr*	12	6

*not recommended

COLORS

Choosing colors can be fun, but sometimes a little difficult. Your project will tell you what yarn colors you will need. When you begin searching for the recommended colors, you may be slightly overwhelmed by the different shades of each color. Here are a few guidelines to consider when choosing your colors.

• Consider where you are going to place the finished project. If the project is going in a particular room in your house, match your yarn to the room's colors.

• Try not to mix very bright colors with dull colors. For example, if you're stitching a project using country colors, don't use a bright Christmas red with country blues and greens. Instead, use a maroon or country red. Likewise, if you are stitching a bright tissue box cover for a child's room, don't use country blue with bright red, yellow, and green.

• Some projects require several shades of a color, such as shades of pink in a flower. Make sure your shades of yarn blend well together.

• Sometimes, you may have trouble finding 3 or 4 shades of a color. If you think your project warrants the extra expense, you can usually find several shades of a color available in tapestry or Persian yarn.

• Remember, you don't have to use the colors suggested in the color key. If you find a blue tissue box cover that you really like, but your house is decorated in pink, change the colors in the tissue box cover to pink!

AMOUNTS

Some projects will list yardages in the project instructions; however, many do not. A handy way of estimating yardages is to make a yarn yardage estimator. Cut a 1 yard piece of yarn for each different stitch used in your project. For each stitch, work as many stitches as you can with the 1 yard length of yarn.

To use your yarn yardage estimator, count the number of stitches you were able to make, say 72 Tent Stitches. Now, look at the chart for the project you want to make. Estimate the number of ecru Tent Stitches on the chart, say 150. Now divide the estimated number of ecru stitches by the actual number stitched with a yard of yarn. One hundred fifty divided by 72 is approximately 2. So you will need about 2 yards of ecru yarn to make your project. Repeat this for all stitches and yarn colors. To allow for repairs and practice stitches, purchase extra yardage of each color. If you have yarn left over, remember that scraps of yarn are perfect for small projects such as magnets or when you need just a few inches of a particular color for another project.

In addition to purchasing an adequate amount of each color of yarn, it is also important to buy all of the yarn you need to complete your project at the same time. Yarn often varies in the amount of dye used to color the yarn. Although the variation may be slight when yarns from two different dye lots are held together, the variation is usually very apparent on a stitched piece.

Each type of yarn used with plastic canvas is pictured in the photo below to show you their differences in width, texture, and sheen. As you can see, the look you want for your project will be a key factor in the type of yarn or thread that you choose. After you've worked with yarn, you might like to experiment with other ways to cover the canvas. Raffia and torn fabric strips can be used to create charming projects. Ribbons and metallic cords are pretty accents and can also be used to cover canvas. Try them all and discover different ways to enjoy plastic canvas.

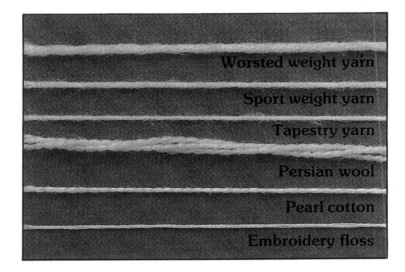

Worsted weight yarn
Sport weight yarn
Tapestry yarn
Persian wool
Pearl cotton
Embroidery floss

 _____ **LESSON #3** _____
SELECTING NEEDLES

TYPES OF NEEDLES

Stitching on plastic canvas should be done with a blunt needle called a tapestry needle. Tapestry needles are sized by numbers; the higher the number, the smaller the needle. The correct size needle to use depends on the canvas mesh size and the yarn thickness. The needle should be small enough to allow the threaded needle to pass through the canvas holes easily, without disturbing canvas threads. The eye of the needle should be large enough to allow yarn to be threaded easily. If the eye is too small, yarn will wear thin and may break.

RECOMMENDED SIZE

The chart below will help you choose the correct needle size for your project.

Mesh	Needle
5	#16 tapestry
7	#16 tapestry
10	#20 tapestry
14	#24 tapestry

PREPARING CANVAS

Before cutting out your pieces, notice the thread count of each piece on your chart. The thread count is usually located above the piece on the chart. The thread count tells you the number of threads in the width and height of the canvas pieces. As you can see on our sample chart, the thread count for the Chicken is 18 x 18 threads. Follow the thread count and cut out a rectangle the specified size. Remember to count threads, not holes. If you accidentally count holes, your piece is going to be the wrong size. If there is room around your chart, it may be helpful to use a ruler and pencil to extend the grid lines of the chart to form a rectangle (see sample chart).

Sample Chart

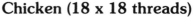

Chicken (18 x 18 threads)

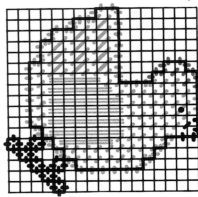

Especially if you are a beginner, you may want to mark the outline of the piece on your canvas. Use a China marker, grease pencil, or fine point permanent marker to draw the outline of your shape on the canvas. Before you begin stitching, be sure to remove all markings with a dry tissue. Any remaining markings are likely to rub off on your yarn as you stitch.

CUTTING CANVAS

A good pair of household scissors is recommended for cutting plastic canvas. However, a craft knife is helpful when cutting a small area from the center of a larger piece of canvas. For example, a craft knife is recommended for cutting the opening out of a tissue box cover top. When using a craft knife, be sure to protect the table below your canvas. A layer of cardboard or a magazine should provide enough padding to protect your table.

When cutting canvas, be sure to cut as close to the thread as possible without cutting into the thread. If you don't cut close enough, "nubs" or "pickets" will be left on the edge of your canvas. Be sure to cut off all nubs from the canvas before you begin to stitch, because nubs will snag the yarn and are difficult to cover.

When cutting plastic canvas along a diagonal, cut through the center of each intersection. This will leave enough plastic on both sides of the cut so that both pieces of canvas may be used *(Fig. 7)*. Diagonal corners will also snag yarn less and be easier to cover.

Fig. 7

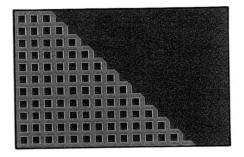

Sometimes the chart will show a slit in the plastic canvas *(Fig. 8)*. To make slits, use a craft knife to cut exactly through the center of an intersection of plastic canvas threads *(Fig. 9)*. Repeat for the number of intersections needed. When stitching the piece, be careful not to carry yarn across slits.

Fig. 8

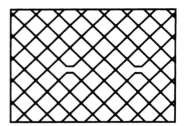

Fig. 9

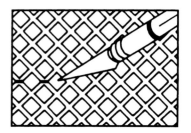

If your project has several pieces, you may want to cut them all out before you begin stitching. Keep your cut pieces in a sealable plastic bag to prevent loss.

LESSON #5
THREADING YOUR NEEDLE

Many people wonder, "What is the best way to thread my needle?" Here are a couple of methods. Practice each one with a scrap of yarn and see what works best for you. There are also several yarn size needle threaders available at your local craft store.

FOLD METHOD

First, sharply fold the end of yarn over your needle; then remove needle. Keeping the fold sharp, push the needle onto the yarn **(Fig. 10)**.

Fig. 10

THREAD METHOD

Fold a 5" piece of sewing thread in half, forming a loop. Insert loop of thread through the eye of your needle **(Fig. 11)**. Insert yarn through the loop and pull the thread back through your needle, pulling yarn through at the same time.

Fig. 11

LESSON #6
LEARNING THE STITCHES

This section is not only designed to teach you the stitches but it will be a helpful reference guide. We've given a brief description along with a step-by-step figure of each stitch. When following a figure, bring your threaded needle up through the canvas at **1** and all **odd** numbers and down through the canvas at **2** and all **even** numbers.

ALTERNATING MOSAIC STITCH

This stitch is made by working Mosaic Stitches in alternating directions **(Fig. 12)**.

Fig. 12

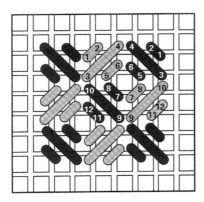

ALTERNATING SCOTCH STITCH

This Scotch Stitch variation is worked over three or more threads, forming alternating blocks as shown in **Fig. 13**.

Fig. 13

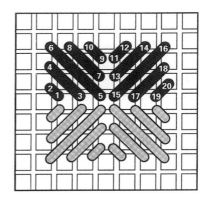

BACKSTITCH

The Backstitch is a versatile stitch which has more than one use. It can be used to completely cover canvas as shown in **Fig. 14**. Backstitch can also be worked over completed stitches to outline features or add details as shown in **Fig. 15**. Sometimes Backstitch is worked over more than one thread when outlining or adding details.

Fig. 14

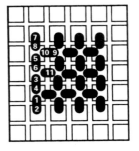

Fig. 15

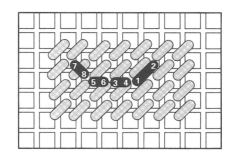

BARGELLO STITCH

This stitch consists of Straight Gobelin Stitches which form a zigzag pattern *(Fig. 16)*.

Fig. 16

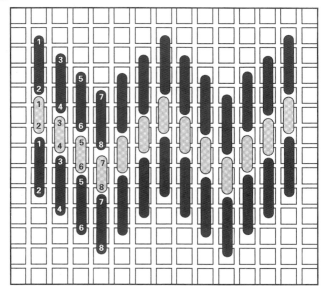

BYZANTINE STITCH

A zigzag effect is created by the Byzantine Stitch. It is composed of Slanting Gobelin Stitches worked in a diagonal pattern as shown in **Fig. 17**. This pattern may slant up to the right or left.

Fig. 17

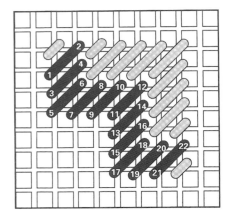

CASHMERE STITCH

This rectangular stitch is formed by working four diagonal stitches as shown in **Fig. 18**.

Fig. 18

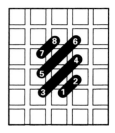

CHECKERED SCOTCH STITCH

This stitch is a combination of Scotch Stitches and Tent Stitches that form a checkerboard pattern *(Fig. 1*

Fig. 19

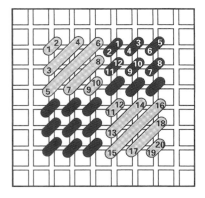

7

CROSS STITCH

This stitch is composed of two stitches (*Fig. 20*). The top stitch of each cross must always be made in the same direction. The number of intersections may vary according to the chart (*Fig. 21*).

Fig. 20

Fig. 21

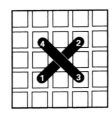

DOUBLE BRICK STITCH

This series of stitches is worked over four threads, forming staggered horizontal rows as shown in **Fig. 22**.

Fig. 22

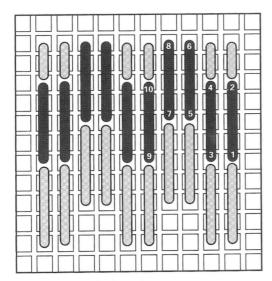

DOUBLE CROSS STITCH

This stitch is used as a decorative stitch. Work stitch as shown in **Fig. 23**.

Fig. 23

DOUBLE LEVIATHAN STITCH

Used for decorative purposes, this stitch is worked over four threads and is composed of eight stitches all crossing at the center (*Fig. 24*).

Fig. 24

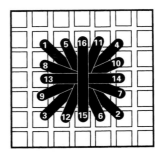

FRENCH KNOT

Bring needle up through hole. Wrap yarn once around needle and insert needle in same hole, holding end of yarn with non-stitching fingers (*Fig. 25*). Tighten knot; then pull needle through canvas, holding yarn until it must be released.

Fig. 25

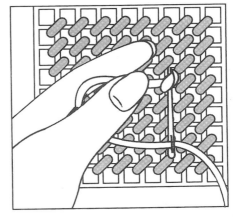

HUNGARIAN DIAMOND STITCH

A variation of the Hungarian Stitch, this series of stitches is worked in horizontal or vertical rows (*Fig. 26*).

Fig. 26

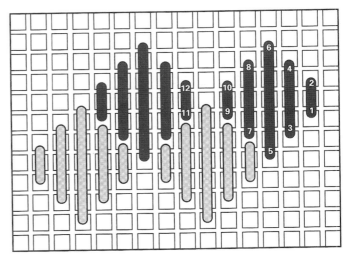

8

LEAF STITCH

This decorative stitch is composed of nine stitches. Start at base of leaf and work clockwise *(Fig. 27)*.

Fig. 27

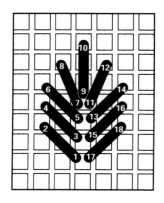

MILANESE STITCH

This diagonal stitch is worked from lower right to upper left as shown in **Fig. 28**.

Fig. 28

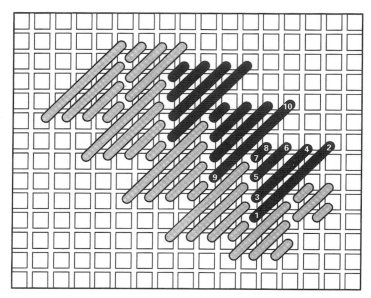

MOSAIC STITCH

This three stitch pattern forms small squares *(Fig. 29)*.

Fig. 29

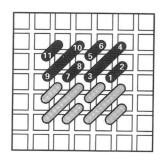

OVERCAST STITCH

This stitch covers the edge of the canvas and joins pieces of canvas *(Fig. 30)*. It may be necessary to go through the same hole more than once to get an even coverage on the edge, especially at the corners.

Fig. 30

PARISIAN STITCH

The Parisian Stitch is a series of stitches worked in horizontal or vertical rows *(Fig. 31)*.

Fig. 31

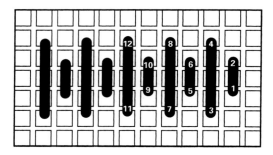

REVERSED TENT STITCH

Like the Tent Stitch, this stitch is worked in vertical or horizontal rows over one intersection as shown in **Fig. 32**. Reversed Tent Stitches always slant up to the left.

Fig. 32

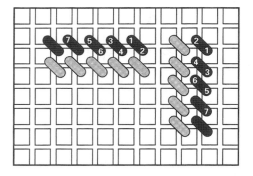

RHODES VARIATION STITCH

This decorative stitch is worked counterclockwise over eight threads (*Fig. 33*).

Fig. 33

ROSE STITCH

To make a Rose, use a 48″ length of yarn. Following **Fig. 34**, form a 5 spoke foundation. Bring needle up at 11 and weave yarn over and under spokes as shown in **Fig. 35**, keeping yarn tension loose. When spokes are covered, pull yarn slightly to puff Rose. With point of needle, pull up petals. Continue weaving until spokes are fully covered. Anchor yarn end on wrong side.

Fig. 34

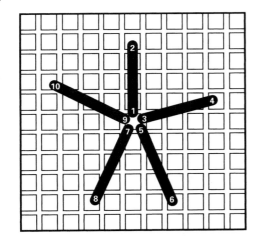

Fig. 35

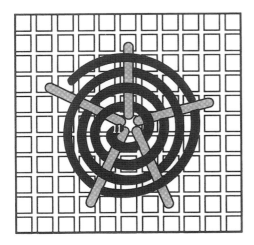

SCOTCH STITCH

This stitch may be worked over three or more threads and forms a square. **Fig. 36** shows it worked over three threads.

Fig. 36

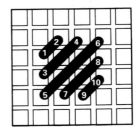

SHELL STITCH

The Shell Stitch consists of three upright stitches drawn together in the middle by a horizontal tie-down stitch. After tying down each shell, work Gobelin Stitches to cover exposed canvas as shown in **Fig. 37**.

Fig. 37

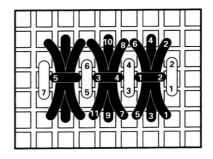

SLANTING GOBELIN STITCH

This stitch covers more than one intersection of threads and may slant in either direction. The number of intersections may vary according to the chart. It may be worked either horizontally or vertically (*Fig. 38*).

Fig. 38

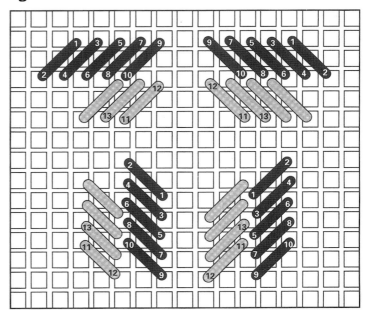

SMYRNA CROSS STITCH

This stitch is worked over two threads as a decorative stitch. Each stitch is worked completely before going on to the next (*Fig. 39*).

Fig. 39

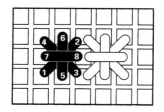

STRAIGHT GOBELIN STITCH

This is a basic straight stitch and is worked over a number of threads rather than intersections. The number of threads may vary according to the chart. It may be worked either horizontally or vertically (*Fig. 40*).

Fig. 40

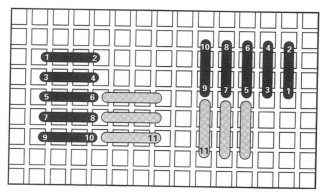

TENT STITCH

This stitch is worked in vertical or horizontal rows over one intersection as shown in **Fig. 41**. Tent Stitches always slant up to the right.

Fig. 41

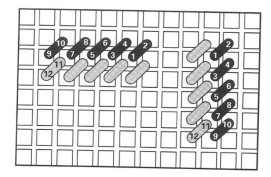

TIED DOUBLE CROSS STITCH

This stitch is worked in three steps with three colors. With first color, work large cross over four threads (*Fig. 42*). Then with second color, work upright cross between large crosses (*Fig. 43*). With third color work upright cross over intersections of large crosses and where large crosses meet (*Fig. 44*).

Fig. 42

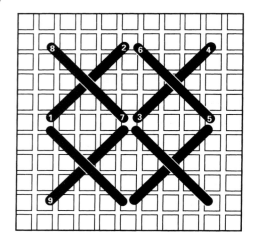

Fig. 43

Fig. 44

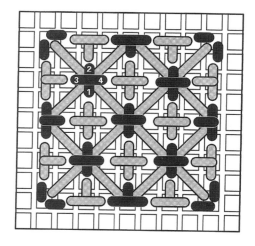

TRIANGLE STITCH

This stitch is formed by working straight stitches to form a triangle. The size of the triangle may vary according to the chart (*Fig. 45*).

Fig. 45

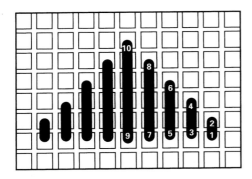

TRIPLE CROSS STITCH

A large Cross Stitch is worked over three horizontal and three vertical threads. Then complete each stitch as shown in **Fig. 46**.

Fig. 46

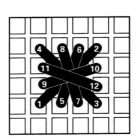

UPRIGHT CROSS STITCH

This stitch is worked over two threads as shown in **Fig. 47**. The top stitch of each cross must always be made in the same direction.

Fig. 47

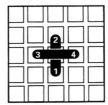

_____ LESSON #7 _____
READING & UNDERSTANDING CHARTS

COLOR KEY

A color key is given with each chart. The key indicates the colors of yarn used and how each is represented on the chart. When ecru yarn is represented by a tan line on the color key, all tan stitches on the chart should be stitched with ecru yarn. All straight stitches are represented by a line in the color key. There are some stitches, such as the French Knot, which cannot be represented by straight lines on the chart. French Knots are represented by dots of color in the color key and chart.

CHART

Whenever possible, the drawing on the chart looks like the completed stitch. For example, the Tent Stitches on the charts are drawn diagonally across one intersection of threads just like a Tent Stitch looks on your piece of plastic canvas. Likewise, Gobelin Stitches on the charts look identical to the Gobelin Stitches on your plastic canvas. When a stitch cannot clearly be drawn on the chart, like a French Knot, a symbol will be used instead as explained in the previous section. If you have difficulty determining what a certain stitch on your chart might be, refer to the Stitches Used section of your instructions.

LESSON #8
STITCHING TECHNIQUES

WHERE TO START

It is best to begin stitching with a piece of yarn that is approximately 1 yard long. However, when working large areas of the same color, you may want to begin with a longer length of yarn to reduce the number of yarn ends and keep the back neat. Don't knot the end of your yarn before you begin stitching! Instead, begin each length of yarn by coming up from the wrong side of canvas and leaving a 1" - 2" tail on the wrong side. Hold this tail against the canvas and work the first few stitches over the tail. When secure, clip tail close to your stitched piece as shown in **Fig. 48**. Clipping the tail close to the stitched piece is very important because long tails can become tangled in future stitches or can show through to the right side of canvas.

Fig. 48

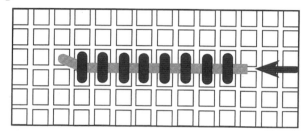

Probably the best place to begin stitching is on one edge of your piece. This eliminates the possibility of accidentally starting in the wrong place by counting incorrectly toward the center of your canvas.

Whenever possible, work white and light areas first so you will not pull fuzz from the completed work into your light areas.

Remember to review any unfamiliar stitches before you begin stitching. Following your chart and stitch diagrams closely, come up through the canvas at one end of the stitch and go down through canvas at opposite end of the stitch. Keep your stitching tension consistent, with each stitch lying flat and even on the canvas. A tight tension is caused by pulling or yanking on the yarn. When the tension is tight, the yarn will be strained and you will be able to see through your stitched piece. Loose tension is caused by not pulling the yarn firmly enough. When the tension is loose, the yarn will not lie flat on the canvas, which will allow canvas threads to show through.

Most stitches tend to twist the working yarn. Drop your needle and let the yarn untwist or roll the needle between thumb and index finger in the opposite direction of the twist every three or four stitches or whenever needed. End your yarn by running your needle through several stitches on the wrong side of the stitched piece. Again, remember to cut yarn tails close to the stitched piece. Continue following the chart and changing colors and stitches as necessary to complete all pieces.

LESSON #9
JOINING PIECES

To indicate where pieces are joined, our charts will often have symbols or placement lines. The instructions will indicate whether pieces are joined by matching edges, symbols, or placement lines.

The Overcast Stitch is the most common stitch used to join edges of canvas pieces together. When joining with the Overcast Stitch, be sure to use an even tension as you join pieces, not too tight or too loose. Also, be sure to completely cover the edges of canvas. This may require stitching through the holes more than once, especially at the corners.

Pieces can be joined in about as many ways as you can imagine. The most common way is joining two or more pieces of canvas along a straight edge. The easiest way to join straight edges is to place one piece on top of the other with right or wrong sides together. Make sure the edges to be joined are even; then stitch the pieces together through all layers.

There may be times when you'll have to join a diagonal edge to a straight edge. The holes of the two pieces will not line up exactly. Just keep pieces even and stitch through holes as many times as necessary to completely cover the canvas.

Sometimes you'll have to join the edge of one piece to an unworked thread in the center of another piece. Simply place one piece on top of the other, matching the indicated threads or symbols. Join by stitching through both layers.

Occasionally a small piece will be attached to a large piece over the completed stitches. For example, a flower shape may be attached to a tissue box cover top. The instructions may indicate to attach the flower with a French Knot or to tack the pieces together. To attach with a French Knot, work the French Knot through both layers of canvas. To tack, come up through bottom piece, catch some of the yarn on the wrong side of the top piece, and go back down through the bottom piece.

LESSON #10
UNDERSTANDING PROJECT INSTRUCTIONS

When you first examine a plastic canvas chart and instructions, there may be a few things that are confusing to you. In this section we'll take you step-by-step through understanding the instructions.

SIZE
The instructions always list the approximate size of the completed project.

Size: 4¾"w x 4¾"h x 2½"d

SUPPLIES
The supply list tells you everything you'll need to complete the project. This includes your canvas, yarn, needle, and any other items needed for the project. The supply list will refer you to the color key for your yarn.

Supplies: One 10⅝" x 13⅝" sheet of 7 mesh plastic canvas, worsted weight yarn (refer to color key), and #16 tapestry needle

STITCHES USED
This section lists every stitch that is used in the project. Review the list of stitches. If there are any stitches that are unfamiliar to you, refer to Lesson #6, pages 6-12, and study the description and figures. Practice the stitch a few times on a scrap of canvas until you are comfortable with it.

Stitches Used: French Knot, Gobelin Stitch, Overcast Stitch, Smyrna Cross Stitch, and Tent Stitch

INSTRUCTIONS
We recommend that you read the entire instructions for a project before you begin working on the project. Then follow the instructions in order as you stitch. For lengthy instructions, we recommend that you use a ruler or highlighter to help you keep your place.

LESSON #11
WASHING INSTRUCTIONS

If you used acrylic yarn for all of your stitches, you may hand wash plastic canvas projects in warm water with a mild detergent. Do not rub or scrub stitches; this will cause the yarn to fuzz. Allow your stitched piece to air dry. Do not put stitched pieces in a clothes dryer. The plastic canvas could melt in the heat of a dryer. Do not dry clean your plastic canvas. The chemicals used in dry cleaning could dissolve the plastic canvas. When the piece is dry, you may need to trim the fuzz from your project with a small pair of sharp scissors.

Now that you've READ all about how to do plastic canvas, it's time to start STITCHING on plastic canvas. The following Coaster Set is designed especially for you to learn lots of stitches and to try your hand at choosing colors. The color keys are only to let you know the placement of shades of color. The color is up to you. And we even broke our own rule and made one Coaster Set all in the same color, just for fun.

Gather your supplies, count your threads, practice your stitches, and have a GREAT TIME! Remember, if you have a problem, you can always go back and review a Lesson.

COASTERS
Size: 4¼"w x 4¼"h each
Supplies: Two 10⅝" x 13⅝" sheets of 7 mesh plastic canvas, worsted weight yarn (refer to color keys and photos), #16 tapestry needle, cork or felt (optional), and clear-drying craft glue for use with cork or felt
Instructions: Follow chart and use required stitches to work Coaster. If backing is desired, cut cork or felt slightly smaller than Coaster and glue to wrong side of stitched piece.

COASTER A

◩ light   ◩ medium   ◩ dark

Coaster A (30 x 30 threads)

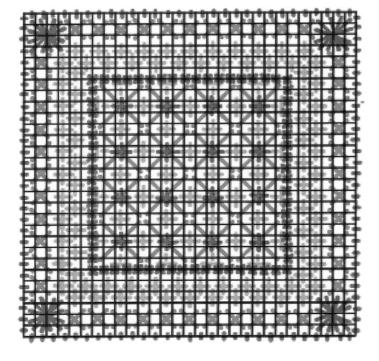

Stitches Used: Cross Stitch, Overcast Stitch, Tied Double Cross Stitch, Triple Cross Stitch, and Upright Cross Stitch

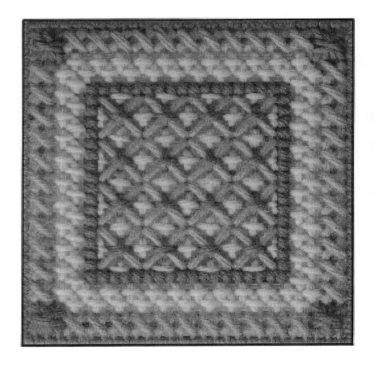

COASTER B

Stitches Used: Mosaic Stitch, Overcast Stitch, Scotch Stitch, and Smyrna Cross Stitch

☑ light   ☑ medium   ☑ dark

Coaster B (30 x 30 threads)

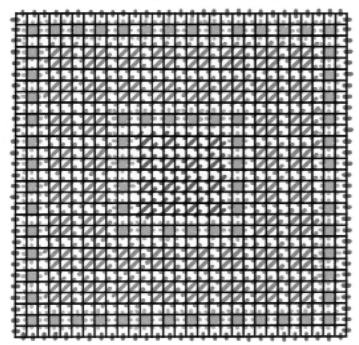

COASTER C

Stitches Used: Double Leviathan Stitch, French Knot, Leaf Stitch, Overcast Stitch, Reversed Tent Stitch, and Tent Stitch

☑ light   ☑ dark
☑ medium   ☑ light Fr. Knot

Coaster C (30 x 30 threads)

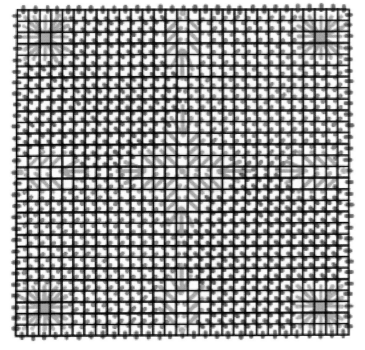

COASTER D

Stitches Used: Alternating Scotch Stitch, Double Cross Stitch, Overcast Stitch, and Slanting Gobelin Stitch

□ light ▨ medium ▨ dark

Coaster D (30 x 30 threads)

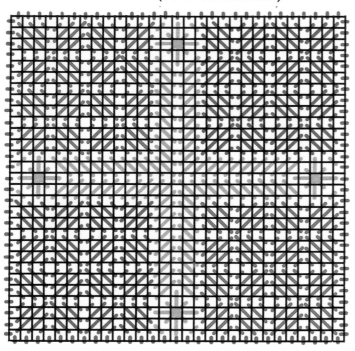

COASTER E

Stitches Used: Alternating Mosaic Stitch, Backstitch, Byzantine Stitch, Milanese Stitch, and Overcast Stitch

▨ light ▨ medium ▨ dark

Coaster E (30 x 30 threads)

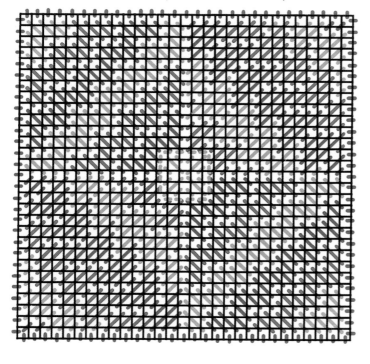

COASTER F

Stitches Used: Cashmere Stitch, Hungarian Diamond Stitch, Overcast Stitch, and Triangle Stitch

☑ light   ☑ medium   ☑ dark

Coaster F (30 x 30 threads)

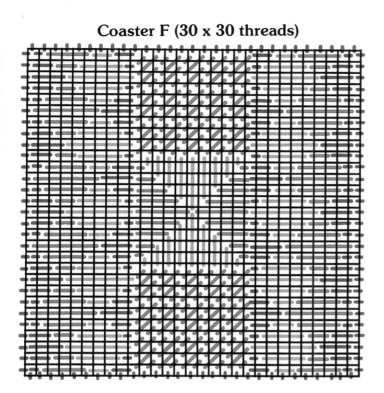

COASTER G

Stitches Used: Bargello Stitch, Checkered Scotch Stitch, Hungarian Diamond Stitch, and Overcast Stitch

☑ light   ☑ medium   ☑ dark

Coaster G (30 x 30 threads)

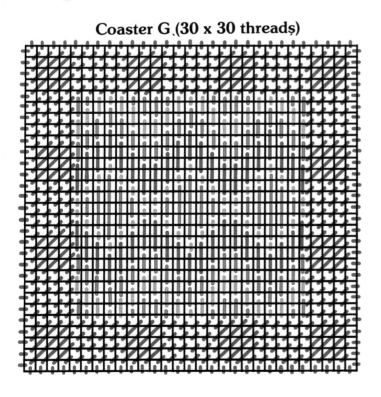

COASTER H

☑ light   ☑ medium   ☑ dark

Stitches Used: Backstitch, Double Brick Stitch, Overcast Stitch, Parisian Stitch, Shell Stitch, and Tent Stitch

Coaster H (30 x 30 threads)

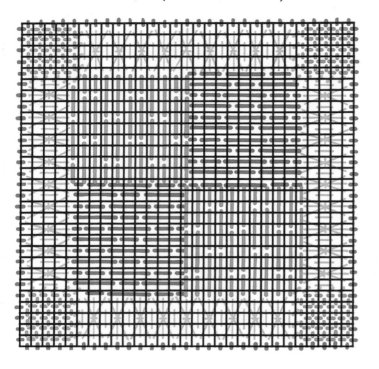

COASTER BOX

Size: 4¾"w x 4¾"h x 2½"d

Supplies: Two 10⅝" x 13⅝" sheets of 7 mesh plastic canvas, worsted weight yarn (refer to color key and photos), and #16 tapestry needle

Stitches Used: Cross Stitch, Leaf Stitch, Overcast Stitch, Reversed Tent Stitch, Rhodes Variation Stitch, Rose Stitch, Straight Gobelin Stitch, and Tent Stitch

Instructions: Follow charts and use required stitches to work Coaster Box pieces. Use light yarn to join pieces. Join Top Sides along short edges. Join Top to Top Sides. Join Bottom Sides along short edges. For Bottom, cut a piece of plastic canvas 32 x 32 threads. *(Note: Bottom is not worked.)* Join Bottom to Bottom Sides.

☑ light   ☑ med C   ☑ dark B
☑ med A   ☑ dark A   ☑ dark C
☑ med B

Top Side (34 x 6 threads) (Work 4)

Bottom Side (32 x 16 threads) (Work 4)

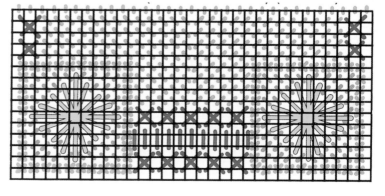

19

Top (34 x 34 threads)

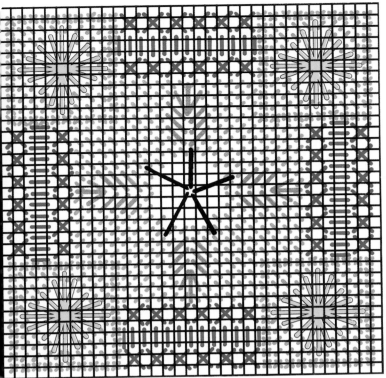

LESSON #13
EXPERIMENTING ON YOUR OWN

Now that you have mastered the basics of working with plastic canvas, you might want to take a project and "customize" it by adding a special design of your own. Or personalize a project with a monogram. You may wish to begin designing your own pieces.

Bookmarks, magnets, coasters, tissue box covers — boundless patterns and projects are just waiting to be created! Use the grid we've provided to come up with your own ideas for unique gifts and projects for your home or office.

We have made every effort to ensure that these instructions are accurate and complete. We cannot, however, be responsible for human error, typographical mistakes, or variations in individual work.

Instructions tested and cover items made by Christel Shelton.